THOMAS EDISON INVENTS THE LIGHT BULB

by Douglas Hustad

Content Consultant
Paul Israel, PhD
Director and General Editor,
Thomas Edison Papers
Rutgers University

Core Library

An Imprint of Abdo Publishing
abdopublishing.com

abdopublishing.com

Published by Abdo Publishing, a division of ABDO, PO Box 398166, Minneapolis, Minnesota 55439. Copyright © 2016 by Abdo Consulting Group, Inc. International copyrights reserved in all countries. No part of this book may be reproduced in any form without written permission from the publisher. Core Library™ is a trademark and logo of Abdo Publishing.

Printed in the United States of America, North Mankato, Minnesota
072015
012016

THIS BOOK CONTAINS
RECYCLED MATERIALS

Cover Photo: Mondadori Portfolio/Getty Images
Interior Photos: Mondadori Portfolio/Getty Images, 1; Schenectady Museum/Hall of Electrical History Foundation/Corbis, 4; Ann Ronan Pictures/Print Collector/Getty Images, 9; ullstein bild/Getty Images, 12; Brady-Handy Collection/Library of Congress, 15; Shutterstock Images, 19 (left); Universal History Archive/Getty Images, 19 (right); AP Images, 20, 32; Red Line Editorial, 24; Time Life Pictures/Mansell/The LIFE Picture Collection/Getty Images, 28, 45; The Print Collector/Getty Images, 34; Fotosearch/Getty Images, 36; Al Willard/NY Daily News Archive/Getty Images, 40

Editor: Arnold Ringstad
Series Designer: Maggie Villaume

Library of Congress Control Number: 2015945849

Cataloging-in-Publication Data
Hustad, Douglas.
 Thomas Edison invents the light bulb / Douglas Hustad.
  p. cm. -- (Great moments in science)
ISBN 978-1-68078-020-8 (lib. bdg.)
Includes bibliographical references and index.
1. Electric lighting--Juvenile literature. 2. Light bulbs--Juvenile literature.
I. Title.
621.3--dc23
                                                                                    2015945849

CONTENTS

CHAPTER ONE
"Paper that a Breath
Would Blow Away"........... **4**

CHAPTER TWO
Becoming the
Wizard of Menlo Park **12**

CHAPTER THREE
Subdividing the Light....... **20**

CHAPTER FOUR
Lighting Up the World....... **28**

CHAPTER FIVE
Bringing It to the Masses.... **36**

Important Dates.................**42**

Stop and Think **44**

Glossary...................... **46**

Learn More....................**47**

Index **48**

About the Author **48**

CHAPTER ONE

"PAPER THAT A BREATH WOULD BLOW AWAY"

y October 1879, the electric light had been Thomas Alva Edison's obsession for months. Day after day, he worked in his laboratory. The subject that occupied most of his thoughts was the filament. This thin wire inside the light bulb glowed to create light. Getting such a delicate object to burn brightly while also lasting a long time was a tough task indeed. His earlier

Edison and his assistants searched for a filament material that would burn bright and last for many hours.

experiments had used filaments of carbon. Often made from paper or cardboard, carbon was cheap and burned well—perhaps too well. These early carbon experiments burned out quickly. They lasted ten to fifteen minutes at the most.

Between late 1878 and October 1879, Edison focused on platinum. He had better results, but they came at a cost. Platinum was very expensive. It did, however, burn hot and bright. Edison showed off his platinum light to reporters, and they were impressed. One *New York Sun* reporter declared, "The strip of platinum that acted as a burner did not burn. It was incandescent. It threw off a light pure and white." Edison boasted of the light's virtues to anyone who would listen. Unlike those fueled by gas, Edison's light did not produce any smoke or dirt. It was the first clean artificial lighting. It was also the first type of lighting that did not produce a flame. But Edison kept one thing secret. His platinum filament light would burn out after only a few hours.

The bulb's short life span was not practical. Edison's light needed to last for several hundred hours. He experimented with ways to make the filament last longer. By removing air from the bulb, Edison was able to get better results. His research showed that air weakened the metal as it was heating. That made it melt faster. Removing the air from the bulb, thereby creating a vacuum, prevented this. But even with that effect, the problem remained: platinum was expensive. Edison sought to find a cheaper source of the metal.

The Moment of Discovery

Frustrated, Edison spent long nights in his laboratory in Menlo Park, New Jersey. The light bulb and the generator needed to power it were not his only projects. Edison was also developing improvements for another invention. His carbon transmitter, created by 1877, had improved audio quality for Alexander Graham Bell's telephone. The carbon material Edison used in the transmitter was called lampblack. It was made from the byproducts of burning kerosene. Edison had much of this material in his lab.

In October 1879, Edison was idly toying with a piece of lampblack while lost in thought. Without realizing it, he'd molded the piece into a fine thread. Seeing what he had made, he was struck with inspiration. He decided to try the lampblack as a new filament. The early tests showed promising results, but it was not an instant success. More experiments were needed.

The telephone Edison worked on was much different from the phones of today.

Fine Tuning

He tried many variations of the same kind of material. Early one morning, Edison and his team tried a carbonized cotton thread molded into a horseshoe shape. The bulb lit up the laboratory for 14 hours. This still was not enough, but it was a huge leap forward.

In November 1879, he applied for a patent for the carbon filament. People were amazed that light came from such a modest source. In December, one

The Global Search for Bamboo

Edison looked across the globe for ways to perfect his invention. After his breakthrough, he tried other carbon filament materials. One that showed a lot of promise was bamboo. Starting in late 1880, Edison sent people all around the world searching for just the right type. One lab worker even died of yellow fever while in Cuba. His replacement traveled to Japan and China. Another went to Brazil and collected many samples. Nothing was as good as one found in Japan. A Japanese farmer agreed to supply Edison with one particular kind of bamboo. This arrangement lasted many years.

reporter described the filament as so delicate, it was like "paper that a breath would blow away."

By the start of 1880, Edison's bulbs were lasting for more than 300 hours. His life, and the world, would never be the same.

This passage appeared in a *New York Herald* article on December 21, 1879:

> *The near approach of the first public exhibition of Edison's long looked for electric light, announced to take place on New Year's Eve at Menlo Park, on which occasion that place will be illuminated with the new light, has revived public interest in the great inventor's work, and throughout the civilized world scientists and people generally are anxiously awaiting the result. . . . The Herald is now, however, enabled to present to its readers a full and accurate account of his work from its inception to its completion. Edison's electric light, incredible as it may appear, is produced from a little piece of paper—a tiny strip of paper that a breath would blow away. Through this little strip of paper is passed an electric current, and the result is a bright, beautiful light, like the mellow sunset of an Italian autumn.*

Source: "Edison's Light." New York Herald. *The Thomas Edison Papers, Rutgers University, December 21, 1879. Web. Accessed May 26, 2015.*

What's the Big Idea?

What is the main idea from this article? What can you tell about the public's reaction to the new invention? Why might people have been so interested in Edison's electric light?

CHAPTER TWO

BECOMING THE WIZARD OF MENLO PARK

Edison grew up in Port Huron, Michigan. He did not have much formal education. He learned mainly from his mother, a former teacher. In 1859, at age 12, Edison got a job with the Grand Trunk Railroad. He often visited a library in Detroit, Michigan. There, Edison read and learned whatever he could. He was especially interested in anything mechanical. One of his interests was the

As a boy Edison took an interest in mechanical objects.

telegraph. The railroads made heavy use of this communications device. Edison made friends with the local telegraph operator wherever he went. It turned out he had a talent for the telegraph. In 1863 he got a job as a telegraph operator in Port Huron. Over the next few years he worked as an operator in several Midwestern cities.

In 1868 he moved to Boston, Massachusetts. There he worked in the telegraph company's home office. He also worked as an inventor on the side. He began developing new telegraph inventions. In 1869 Edison moved to New York. There he worked on stock ticker technology. By 1872 he was working as an inventor for the telegraph company, and by 1876 he had earned enough money to build his own laboratory in Menlo Park. Edison planned to produce a minor invention every ten days. He would create major inventions every six months.

In 1877 Edison was working on improvements to Alexander Graham Bell's recent invention, the

Edison's phonograph made him a famous inventor.

telephone. He discovered a way of recording sound and playing it back. The machine was known as the phonograph, an early type of record player. This invention made him world famous. It earned him the nickname, "The Wizard of Menlo Park."

Early Lighting Methods

Artificial light was common by the 1700s. However, it was nothing like lights today. Before Edison, all artificial lighting required a flame. Houses and streets were lighted either with burning oil or grease. Soon, gaslights became the wave of the future. Gas for lighting could be delivered directly to homes through pipes from a central location. Edison later modeled his system after this principle. He would run wires for his lights from a central power station. By 1804 the first gas lighting company was in business in London. One-quarter of Americans had access to gas lighting by the 1840s. Artificial lighting was cheaper than ever.

But gas had many downsides. Each lamp had to be lighted and put out individually. And the lamps gave off chemicals, such as ammonia and sulfur. Outdoors, these chemicals made lights dirty. They made it necessary to clean the lights frequently. But indoors, the toxic fumes turned walls black and made people sick. Electricity did not have these dangers.

Electric Light Progress

Many inventors had tried and failed to invent the electric light. Research on the subject went back decades. For 40 years before Edison, scientists and inventors from all over the world had tried to master it. Edison himself had briefly toyed with the idea in 1877 but had no success.

The latest lighting technology of Edison's time was the arc light. Arc lights were very different from incandescent lights. Both ran on electricity. But incandescent light came from a heated filament that glowed. Arc lights gave off light from a burning "arc" between two pieces of carbon. They gave off a bright light, but the carbon rods had to be moved closer together as they burned. The gap

The Competition

In the fall of 1878, Edison was working hard on the electric light. At the same time, Charles Brush was developing improved arc lights. Brush had designed a system to automatically maintain the gap between the carbon pieces of an arc light. This made it much less work to operate one. Brush later sold his system to private citizens and businesses. It was very bright, and it was most commonly used outdoors. Arc lighting was a major competitor to gas for street lighting in the late 1870s.

between the carbon had to constantly be adjusted to maintain the arc. The carbon eventually would burn out completely. Then it had to be replaced and relit. The high brightness of arc lights made them unsuitable for indoor use.

Inspiration

In September 1878, Edison got a firsthand look at arc lighting. University of Pennsylvania Professor George Baker invited his friend Edison to see the work of William Wallace. Wallace owned a brass foundry in Connecticut. There, Wallace was experimenting with

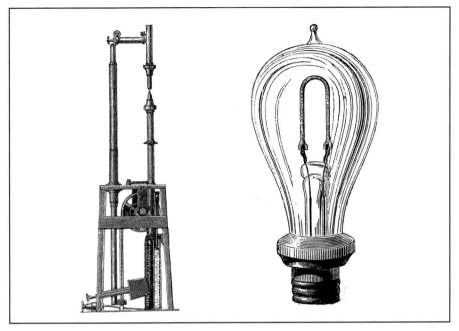

The Two Electric Lights Side by Side
Here you can see Edison's light, *right*, in comparison with a common design of an arc light, *left*. What major differences do you notice? Do you notice any major differences between Edison's bulb and the light bulbs in your home today?

arc lighting. He had a series of eight arc lights running on a power source called a dynamo.

Edison was fascinated. He particularly loved the dynamo. It was much better than the batteries of the time. He now believed he knew how to perfect his light. All he had to do was design a better bulb. Edison's competitive nature took over.

CHAPTER THREE

SUBDIVIDING THE LIGHT

E dison was impressed by Wallace's dynamo. He even got one for his own experiments. Edison believed, though, that arc lighting was not practical for indoor use. Nor would it ever be used on a large scale. It was too bright, hard to operate, and unsafe. Edison continued his work on incandescence. This meant heating a material to the point where it glowed with a bright white color.

Unlike arc lighting, Edison's light was soft enough to be used indoors.

Incandescent light was much softer than arc lighting. It was much more suitable for use in the home.

Softening the intensity of light was called "subdividing." Edison wanted to not only soften the light, but also establish a network of lights. The immense cost of the parts, including the copper used for wiring, made this goal seem impossible. To reduce costs and make his network possible, he needed a lamp with high electrical resistance.

This would enable him to use smaller copper conductors in the system. Many people doubted this could be done. This doubt only encouraged Edison in his work. Now he focused on finding the right filament, creating a vacuum in the bulb, and making a useful circuit.

The Multiple Arc

Edison wanted to use a different type of circuit from the ones used in arc lighting. When arc lights were arranged in a series, they were all connected to each other. The power flowed through every light from beginning to end. If one light went out, they all went out. This would not work for everyday use.

Edison arranged his lights in a multiple arc system. This arrangement is also known as a parallel circuit. It worked like a ladder. Two conductors ran along the outside. Then the lights were placed like rungs on the ladder. If one went out, power kept flowing to every other light. This gave Edison an advantage over arc lighting.

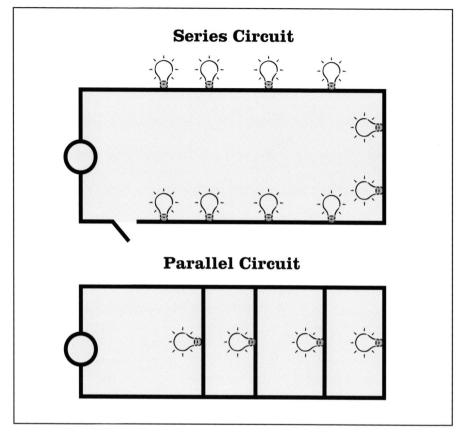

Series Circuit

Parallel Circuit

The Ladder and the Series

These two drawings show the two types of circuits used in Edison's time. The series circuit is how arc lights were arranged. The other is Edison's parallel, ladder-shaped circuit. How do these illustrations help you understand how Edison's work with circuits improved the usefulness of electric lights?

Declaring Victory

Only a week after visiting Wallace, Edison was confident. "I have it!" he declared to a *New York Sun* reporter. His bulb was not perfect, but he knew he was on the right track. After a positive article in the *Sun*, Edison got more attention.

The general public was interested in Edison's inventions. Investors saw an opportunity to make money. Edison and his investors founded the Edison Electric Light Company on October 16, 1878. People lined up to get their share of such an important invention.

Edison knew he needed the money. But he was not excited about the process. Going around to ask investors for funding took him out of the lab. Eventually he insisted investors come to him. He had plenty of work to do. His bulb still did not burn long enough. His lights lasted only a few hours.

A Viable Example

Edison needed to show progress. He was still searching for a filament. In the fall of 1879, his team tried hundreds of options. They went from platinum to lampblack to cotton threads.

The Strangest Filament of All

Edison tried many different filament materials. But one was more unusual than all the others. Two lab workers volunteered hair from their beards to be tested. The others would then place bets on whose beard would last the longest. The competition inspired good-natured debates on whose beard was best.

Carbon had been proven as a suitable filament. The experimentation continued. But Edison now finally had something he could show to the world. "The electric light is perfected," Edison told the *New York Times*. But it would still be more than a year before it was commercially available.

Frank Lewis Dyer, a friend and lawyer of Edison's, wrote about Edison's filament breakthrough in his book *Edison: His Life and Inventions*:

> *This slender, fragile, tenuous thread of brittle carbon, glowing steadily and continuously with a soft light agreeable to the eyes, was the tiny key that opened the door to a world revolutionized in its interior illumination. It was a triumphant vindication of Edison's reasoning powers, his clear perceptions, his insight into possibilities, and his inventive faculty, all of which had already been productive of so many startling, practical, and epoch-making inventions. And now he had stepped over the threshold of a new art which has since become so world-wide in its application as to be an integral part of modern human experience.*

> Source: Frank Lewis Dyer. "Edison: His Life and Inventions." Gutenberg Project. Gutenberg Project, January 26, 2013. Web. Accessed May 27, 2015.

Point of View

Compare and contrast this passage with the excerpt from the *New York Herald* article on page 11, which was written by a neutral observer. How are they different? Similar? What can you tell about why people admired Edison?

CHAPTER FOUR

LIGHTING UP THE WORLD

By December 1879, Edison was ready to unveil his bulb. He planned a New Year's Eve display for the public. The *New York Herald* article announcing the display appeared on December 21. People began to flock to Menlo Park. The Pennsylvania Railroad scheduled special trains to run there.

Edison's laboratory became the site of demonstrations of his new bulb.

Thousands of people came out for the December 31 exhibition. Edison had demonstrations set up all over the lab. People could see the light up close. Edison himself was an attraction. He was already a celebrity inventor at age 32.

Edison kept the lab open to the public on New Year's Day as well. Reporters and everyday citizens alike were thrilled. But Edison still faced the criticism that he could light only his own lab. People wanted to see the lights out on streets and in their homes.

Edison tested his lights on a steamship in May 1880. They performed well. The steamship was not where Edison wanted his lights. He wanted to develop a distribution system to light up homes across the nation. But Edison was eager to show off his invention. Competition in the electric light industry was heating up. Another inventor, William Sawyer, was accusing Edison of stealing his ideas. There was also a New York company making bulbs similar to Edison's. Edison needed to work quickly.

The "Streets" of Menlo Park

Edison wanted to install streetlights in Menlo Park. The only problem was that Menlo Park had hardly any real streets. It was rural and far from the city lights. So Edison set up grids of wires among the open fields. More than five miles (8 km) of wire were laid underground for hundreds of streetlights. It was an outdoor extension of the lab.

Edison planned a demonstration for New York City officials on December 20, 1880. On the same night, Charles Brush was planning to

PERSPECTIVES
The Challenger

Like many Americans, William Sawyer was amazed reading about Edison's carbon filament. But Sawyer was amazed for a different reason. He believed Edison stole his ideas. The men challenged each other back and forth about whose bulb would work. The battle eventually ended up in the courts. The United States Patent Office awarded the patent for a horseshoe-shaped paper carbon filament to Sawyer in 1885. By then it mattered little. Edison had moved beyond carbonized paper for his lamps.

31

Bringing electric lights indoors was Edison's goal, and
New York City was where he could achieve this.

of the New York project. He needed to be in the city to oversee it. The company went ahead with the plan.

By early 1881, Edison was spending most of his time at the company's building in New York. Edison would miss the peace and quiet of Menlo Park. But New York was where he would complete his vision.

EXPLORE ONLINE

Chapter Four talks about Edison demonstrating his light to the public. Not only was this a new invention, it was something people would someday be able to buy. The article at the website below discusses some of the demonstrations that took place. How are these similar or different from how products are demonstrated or sold today? What things do people look for in a new product?

Light Bulb Demonstrations
mycorelibrary.com/light-bulb

CHAPTER FIVE

BRINGING IT TO THE MASSES

Edison kept pushing through competitors, challenges, and politics. He was close to achieving his vision: lighting up New York. But he needed a bigger, city-sized power system. He purchased two buildings on Pearl Street with the intention of making the first central power station. Edison worked long hours getting the station ready.

Edison's workers dug trenches for cables under New York City streets to bring power to electric lights in other buildings.

He sometimes slept there. His workers began laying cables in April 1881.

Work was slow. Edison did not have much to show except for some wires in the ground. Meanwhile, arc lights were still being installed all over the city. And the public still had safety concerns about electricity. The gas light industry spread rumors about it to scare people.

Edison again called on the newspapers to spread his good word. He declared in May 1882 that gas lighting would be completely gone in a few years. He also boasted about his company's experience and history with electricity. Edison got a publicity boost later that year when he installed a lighting system for J. P. Morgan. Morgan was an

Edison's Family

Edison's first wife, Mary, passed away in 1884. They had two sons and a daughter. Edison remarried to Mina Miller in 1886. They had three more children. One of their sons, Charles, became governor of New Jersey. Thomas Alva Edison passed away on October 18, 1931.

influential businessman. He had invested in Edison's company.

Flipping the Switch

On September 4, 1882, at 3:00 p.m., Edison's vision came true. The lights of his first customers buzzed to life. At first, the numbers were small. There were only a few hundred lights. By the end of December, there were 240 customers and 5,000 lights.

It had taken four years and nearly $500,000 to get to this point. Edison had accomplished much.

PERSPECTIVES
The Early Adopter

While J. P. Morgan was on vacation, he had a radical idea. He would use his home to showcase the electric light. Edison installed a generator and system of lights in the New York City mansion. Morgan was thrilled with it. But his neighbors were not. The generator made a lot of noise. One night while the Morgan family attended an opera, a fire broke out. The electricity had caused it. But Morgan did not have the generator removed. Instead, he demanded a new system be installed. The new one worked flawlessly for years. "I hope the Edison Company appreciate the value of my house as an experimental station," Morgan joked.

Electric lighting changed New York City and the world forever.

But the work was not finished. His company worked to expand the network. It also improved the bulbs themselves.

Flipping that first switch was only the beginning. Before long the gas lighting industry, which was worth $400 million in 1882, was gone. In 1889 Edison's companies merged to form Edison General Electric. Three years later, the new company merged with a competitor. It shortened its name to General Electric. That company exists to this day. Edison had successfully introduced electric light, and he helped spread it throughout the world.

FURTHER EVIDENCE

Chapter Five covers Edison's challenges and ultimate success at bringing his lights to people in New York. What was one of the main points of this chapter? What evidence is included to support this point? Read the article at the website below. Does the information in the article support the evidence in this chapter? Does it present new evidence?

The Thomas Edison Papers
mycorelibrary.com/light-bulb

IMPORTANT DATES

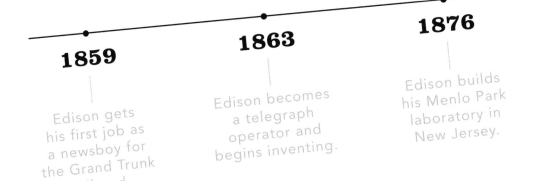

1859

Edison gets his first job as a newsboy for the Grand Trunk Railroad.

1863

Edison becomes a telegraph operator and begins inventing.

1876

Edison builds his Menlo Park laboratory in New Jersey.

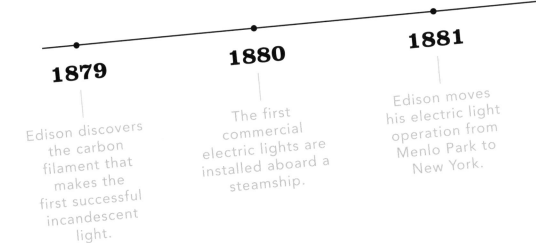

1879

Edison discovers the carbon filament that makes the first successful incandescent light.

1880

The first commercial electric lights are installed aboard a steamship.

1881

Edison moves his electric light operation from Menlo Park to New York.

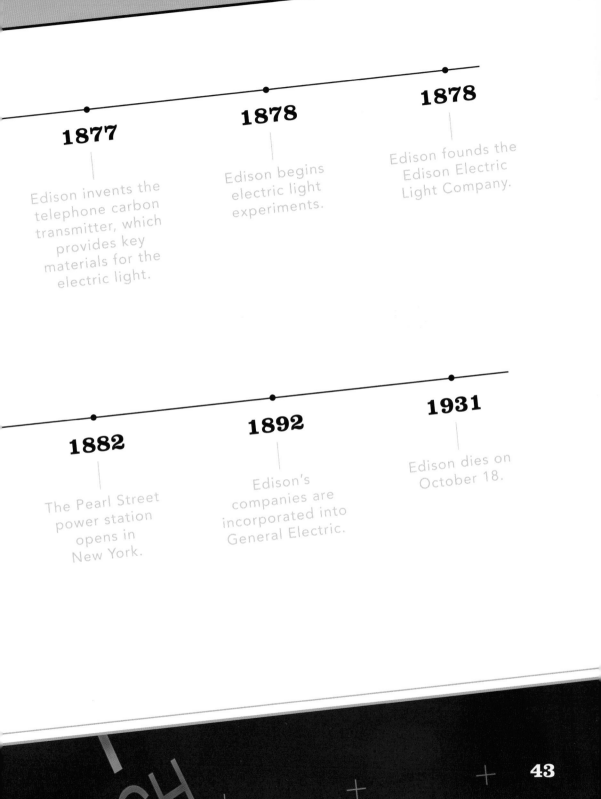

1877

Edison invents the telephone carbon transmitter, which provides key materials for the electric light.

1878

Edison begins electric light experiments.

1878

Edison founds the Edison Electric Light Company.

1882

The Pearl Street power station opens in New York.

1892

Edison's companies are incorporated into General Electric.

1931

Edison dies on October 18.

STOP AND THINK

Tell the Tale

Chapter Four discusses Edison demonstrating his light to the public. Put yourself in the mind of a person from the late 1800s. Write a 200-word diary entry about what it might be like to see an Edison light for the very first time. What questions would you have?

Surprise Me

Chapter One discusses a key moment in Edison's work on the light bulb: the discovery of a useful filament material. After reading this book, what surprised you most about how Edison perfected the light bulb? Write a few sentences about what facts were different from what you had previously thought.

Dig Deeper

After reading this book, what questions do you still have about the history of the light bulb? With an adult's help, find a few reliable sources that can help answer your questions. Write a paragraph about what you learned.

Say What?

Studying inventions can mean learning a lot of new vocabulary. Find five words in the book you've never heard before. Use a dictionary to find out what they mean. Then write the meanings in your own words, and use each new word in a sentence.

GLOSSARY

carbon
a naturally occurring element present in all organic life

circuit
the path through which electricity flows

conductor
a material that electricity can flow through

foundry
a type of factory that produces metal castings

incandescent
heating a material to the point that it glows white

investor
somebody who contributes money to a business

laboratory
a specially designed space for scientific experiments

patent
a legal protection preventing an invention being stolen

phonograph
a type of early record player

platinum
a naturally occurring element that is a rare and expensive metal

transmitter
a device that converts sound into electricity, as in a telephone

vacuum
an enclosed space in which all air has been removed

LEARN MORE

Books

Barretta, Gene. *Timeless Thomas: How Thomas Edison Changed Our Lives.* New York: Henry Holt, 2012.

Frith, Margaret. *Who Was Thomas Alva Edison?* New York: Grosset & Dunlap, 2005.

Pedersen, Charles E. *Thomas Edison.* Edina, MN: Abdo Publishing Company, 2007.

Websites

To learn more about Great Moments in Science visit **booklinks.abdopublishing.com**. These links are routinely monitored and updated to provide the most current information available.

Visit **mycorelibrary.com** for free additional tools for teachers and students.

INDEX

arc lights, 17–19, 21–23, 32, 38

Baker, George, 18
Bell, Alexander Graham, 8, 14
Boston, Massachusetts, 14
Brush, Charles, 18, 31

childhood, 13–14
circuits, 23–24

Dyer, Frank Lewis, 27
dynamo, 19, 21

Edison Electric Light Company, 25, 33

family, 38
filaments
  carbon, 6, 8–9, 10, 26, 27, 31
  platinum, 6–7, 25

gaslights, 6, 16, 18, 38, 41

incandescent lights, 6, 17, 22

Menlo Park, New Jersey, 8, 11, 14, 22, 29, 31, 33, 35
Michigan, 13, 33
Morgan, J. P., 38–39

New York City, 14, 30, 31, 33, 35, 37, 39, 41
news stories, 10, 11, 24–25, 26, 38

patents, 9, 31
phonographs, 15
public demonstrations, 11, 17, 29–31, 33

Sawyer, William, 30, 31

telegraphs, 14
telephones, 8, 15

Upton, Francis R., 22

Wallace, William, 18, 21, 24

ABOUT THE AUTHOR

Douglas Hustad is a children's writer from Minneapolis, Minnesota. He has authored several science books for young people.